Confessions, Inspirations, and Truth

Sharondla Patrice Harvey

1

Credits

Editor

Mr. Alex Culbreth

Cover Designer

Dr. Terrence Cruger

Photographer Credit

Dedication

This book is dedicated to my beautiful daughter. I leave you with these words of sentiment titled Bond.

A bond is a relationship that should never need to be reevaluated every three to six months because you are being filled with untruths or mistold cons.

Bond you say, ours isn't strong but how can it be when you're listening to those who pursue the wrong in me then you respond with the disrespect because you feel it's reject.

Not knowing the hurt you place inside of me that creates a seed of envy. Currency and gifts is what I feel I am used for. I fight within myself saying Lord, what else?

Those same individuals who are silently and sneakily in your ear are the same people who are not complete nor humble and can't even hold their own in times of trouble, but yet still want our bond to crumble.

Uneasy conversations we have make me feel like just saying go ahead believe words of others because you

4

will never have another mother nor another someone who bends over backwards, supports every dream no matter how mean your tone of voice can seem. Words at times are just not enough to fight back the harm those have placed on us. One day you will see those individuals aren't really what they pretend to be.

Falling towards me after you have discovered people, no matter whom they are not who they seemed to be.

Breaking bonds within your mind only because I will no longer let them into mine. I hopefully pray soon you will see it wasn't me instead the limitless encounters of my enemies.

Bond I will never break even though my heart aches. Bonds aren't meant to be one-sided or divided so be strong, open your eyes, and focus on the truth of what you see in thee.

A bond that's truly divine can never be infiltrated by any of Satan's lies nor tries. Bonds aren't broken by conversations one doesn't understand instead of repeating jokes that one can't comprehend.

Wisdom with understanding soon will follow if you allow your hearts not to be hollow. Remain open minded not like those whom fill your thoughts with misguidance.

Listen along with visual proof to see if those people are honest with you. Over time you will see just how jealousy will create envy.

Some day you will see a mother's bond isn't always easily achieved. Wishfully praying, "Is this what seeds can be, obligated to me?" Knowing very well if flee like those whispering obscene tales of me they could never provide the skills God gave to me.

Bonds keep it close and dear because when it's gone there is much to fear. Bond of a Mother.

Contents

Dedication

Introduction

Poems

Journal Thoughts

Author's Favorite Quotes

Family Tribute

Conclusion

About the Author

Author's Contact Page

~ Introduction ~

Have you ever found yourself wanting to confess something to someone knowing that you can inspire them and allow them to be freed from the shackles of life?

Confessions, Inspirations, and Truth is a collection of poetry from the Author that depicts her personal truths as they flow intensely from her soul. The poems will portray her journey through life as she is traveling through episodes of crisis, emotions, trials, tribulations, triumphs, hurt, and pain. The transparency released through her writings will awaken the consciousness of the readers to help them to personally connect and relate with each topic presented.

When one confesses the innermost part of their soul, there is a certain level of inspiration that will be released allowing the reader to receive clarity and insight into their own personal life.

This book will release the truths and perspectives of the Author as she allows the innocence of her soul to be explored and her truths to be discovered and ingested into the hearts and minds of those who read her treasure of poetic ensembles.

I would ask that you sit back and take a personal journey through this poetic experience.

For I will be merciful to their unrighteousness, and their sins and their iniquities will I remember no more.

Hebrews 8:12

Don't Need

I don't need you to get mad when I speak what's
on my mind
Ooh but when you do it
It's just fine
I don't need someone who only feels what they feel
when it comes to mine
you complain every time
Why do I got to be one that's different just because
I don't read between the lines
I don't need to feel like I can't be me when I'm
around you
I thought you were sound proof
I don't need you if I can't call you my own
I don't need you if I can't be completely free of
show ins what's inside of thee
I don't need the mind games or the hook ups with
old flames
I don't need the get them if you can moments
or if nothing comes up in their plans moments
I need the come and take my hand moments
We can conquer the land moments
I'll see if I can go sneak away
I need you to stay
I don't need to give you my heart only for you to
break it apart
I don't need you to make me moan

HELL

I can do that on my own
I don't need to walk your path
I'm carrying my own wrath
I don't need you to come into my life for a season
or any negative reasons
That's like an act of treason
I don't need you if you can't joke
I don't need you to be up then down
I don't need you to see life your way

GOSH

I surely can't stay
I don't need to be silent anymore, time to walk out
the door
I don't need to hurt
I don't need to cry
I shouldn't have to lie
I don't need to pretend about what's going on
within just so you can be my friend
A friend that at any minute can be a foe
I don't need! I don't need! I don't need!
Anyone that doesn't accept ME!
I don't need your whys or lies......
I don't need for you to get close to me but won't
get to know me
I don't need to waste your time or mine

~ Journal Thoughts ~

"Don't Need"

_____
_____
_____
_____
_____
_____
_____
_____
_____
_____
_____
_____
_____
_____
_____
_____
_____
_____
_____
_____

So do not fear, for I am with you;
do not be dismayed, for I am
your God.
I will strengthen you and help you;
I will uphold you with my
righteous right hand.

Isaiah 41:10

Lodebari

Lodebari a space where I cannot speak nor dream
or scream

Lodebari how many of us are trapped it's like time
has relapsed

Patterns of the past that seem to last in the
thoughts of those individuals who will never lift
you up from the demons of the past

Lodebari I refuse to be in your presence again

my life is filled with fields of seed and great deeds
not greed

But with growth which empowers my spirit every
waking minute

Lodebari, Lodebari, Lodebari I have come too far to
remain the same in the thoughts of my mind frame
it's just too hard to explain in Jesus' name........

~ Journal Thoughts ~
"Lodebari"

_____
_____
_____
_____
_____
_____
_____
_____
_____
_____
_____
_____
_____
_____
_____
_____
_____
_____
_____

*Through wisdom is a house built;
and by understanding, it is
established:*

*And by knowledge shall the
chambers be filled with all precious
and pleasant riches.*

*A wise man is strong; yea, a man of
knowledge increaseth strength.*

Proverbs 24:3-5

I CAN'T BREATHE- FREEDOM

I can't breathe is a phrase heard too many times
Law enforcement says it lies
Kneeling on one knee to show the world
we all deserve to be treated equally
Black and Brown people come on take this stand with
me
It's justice, justice, justice that we seek
Change is what it should be in the land of FREE
Instead of the chains they want at my feet
Wait. STOP..... Officer what did I do wrong besides
being born black in a world of wrongs
Laughing Out Loud
I'm black and proud
It's taught it's okay to be white and taunt blacks
but when the roles are reversed blacks are the worse
Freedom is the dream of Martin Luther King
Hmmm..... It remains to be seen when those
FREEDOM bells are actually going to ring
Equality is supposed to be for all not with the white
caucus want it all.....
George Floyd, Trayvon Martin, Breonna Taylor,
Tamir Rice
I will continue to write and fight for our black rights
I can't breathe, I can't breathe
never do I want my daughter to see....
Masks on our face won't prevent the RACE

It just discriminates
CEOs now want to speak out
But when we needed a home or loan you only gave
me doubt
Republicans or Democrats just want to distract us,

the people, from facts
Question?
What good is it to have white privilege when the
image is used for vengeance
not to mention the unfair sentences my people are
given
Which causes relentless repentance
smh.... what a shame is my own people have to vote
for a change
Instead we point fingers at those of us who truly fight
for change
No, they rather stand in line to get the latest gold
chain
Justice, Equality, and Freedom should be granted to
all not just when one of us falls
Falls on the hands and knees of a person
that only sees color....
Stand up, Speak out I'm talking to all of America's
people.......
How many of you remember Medgar Evers?
I didn't, my brother, continue to rock in heaven
The 13th amendment a set of laws that put black's
backs against the walls

"The birth of a nation" only caused us demotion.....
Don't I have the right to breathe?
Don't I have the right to vote?
Don't I have the right to succeed?
Don't I have the right to protest
for my given civil rights without you telling me to
calm down?
You're not white.......
What gets to be 13 if we are created in his image
why aren't we treated equally like the GODS we are
meant to be........
I can't breathe
Step up, Speak out, protest, march, come together
Love each other no matter what color.....

~ Journal Thoughts ~

"I CAN'T BREATHE- FREEDOM"

_____

_____

_____

_____

_____

_____

_____

_____

_____

_____

_____

_____

_____

_____

_____

_____

_____

_____

_____

_____

_____

_____

The LORD is my shepherd; I shall not want.

He maketh me to lie down in green pastures: he leadeth me beside the still waters.

He restoreth my soul: he leadeth me in the paths of righteousness for his name's sake.

Yea, though I walk through the valley of the shadow of death, I will fear no evil: for thou art with me; thy rod and thy staff they comfort me.

Thou preparest a table before me in the presence of mine enemies: thou anointest my head with oil; my cup runneth over.

Surely goodness and mercy shall follow me all the days of my life: and I will dwell in the house of the LORD forever.

Psalm 23

Suffering in Silence

I can't seem to find the words
that explain how I feel inside without using verbs
I wonder if I tell how I feel
will the heart remain real and not become steel?
Not steel as in strength but steal as not exist
Suffering in silence is just a mist suffering in violence
I want to tell you so bad that I miss the love we had
In times when we should have talked, we walked
The silence has gotten so loud between us our minds
can't adjust
Long enough for us to discuss
the disgusts and distrusts we have between us
Suffering In Silence...
Why are we doing this to ourselves
words unread on the bookshelves
Open me up and you will find all the hurt I hide
behind
Then I realized I declined by not speaking my mind
about what's going on inside so I declined but I
survived
Using my body as a way to communicate
It was fake
because I couldn't relate to my mate
Reaching out to you
No response

This is how we got this way
The blocks
Hoping the silence will become sound
then someday we can speak aloud
those precious vows ...
Whenever we are apart it damn near stops my heart
Thinking if we both were smart we wouldn't be at
this part
Suffering in silence .....

~ Journal Thoughts ~
"Suffering in Silence"

_____

_____

_____

_____

_____

_____

_____

_____

_____

_____

_____

_____

_____

_____

_____

_____

_____

_____

_____

_____

For God so loved the world, that he gave his only begotten Son, that whosoever believeth in him should not perish, but have everlasting life.

John 3:16

LOVE

Listen-Observe-Voice-Express

Love, I see you staring in my face
That look will never be replaced
Love is all so sweet
I'm afraid if we meet
I may not know how to receive you
LOVE
God knows it feels like heaven sent from above
Love, trying so hard to grab my attention
when at times I don't mention
Love why can't I see you
Love, you came in my life but at a dangerous price
Love, you're asking me to surrender
but my heart is tender
From a love I thought I had
It wasn't all bad or even sad
Love, you do everything so great if you could you'll
take my fate
Love, it wants to give it like it's given to me but it's
too much hate within me
Not for you LOVE just wondering if love is what it
really was
Love, what does this truly mean, another four letter
word we now use as a meme?
Love, I see it all in your eyes
it's no surprise
How easily it flows in hopes one day I'll grow
LOVE
It hurts so deep at night I cannot sleep

Love, you touch my body and mind
is it what's really inside
Love I see you....
Love, I see the pain it brings to you
How can you love what's not true?
Love you deserve so much more
Love, you say people will kill you, but is this god's
will for you?
Love should be formed in time
not a play button to push forward or rewind
I see you LOVE....
It's more than skin deep
Love, if you could, you'd take my soul
Not to harm, to charm
Love, I'm sorry I'm still blue
Love makes me feed what's real
Love, I want to love you too
Love, I love you back but I slack
I want to give you all of thee
It's so much I reap
A seed I planted of my own left a heart of stone
It's hard to replace or erase the emotions that's been
placed
knowing LOVE is where it begins
Love, you are never unnoticed
Love, you're the diagnosis

LOVE

~ Journal Thoughts ~

"Love"

And I am no more worthy to be called thy son: make me as one of thy hired servants.

And he arose, and came to his father. But when he was yet a great way off, his father saw him, and had compassion, and ran, and fell on his neck, and kissed him.

And the son said unto him, Father, I have sinned against heaven, and in thy sight, and am no more worthy to be called thy son.

But the father said to his servants, Bring forth the best robe, and put it on him; and put a ring on his hand, and shoes on his feet:

Luke 15:19-22

Toxic Tear Drops

These tear drops that fall from my eyes keep

my heart beat in an up rise
Remembering those good times we had that
we both pretend to hide
Oh my those Toxic Tear Drops falling from my
eyes
It was good while it lasted
Wow such a blast from the past
Some may wonder why toxic tear drops
when all they do is make you blinder only in a
sense that will make you wiser
Toxic Tear Drops.......
You took my heart from the start
stole everything that made me whole
I found myself loving you more than me and
I lost that light that grew inside of me
My self-confidence wasn't blooming I agree
It felt like at times I was an abductee
but it was just absence that grew
Toxic Tear Drops........
This I guarantee I will never let those feelings
come back near me
There was a war brewing inside of me that
kept me from seeing the love you had for me
Even though I knew there were things you

hid
I just sit back and tried to live
Toxic Tear Drops

31

I no longer have them fall from my eyes
Why? Because now I can live my life with
pride
One day we will see if we were truly meant to
be
They say if you love something let it go even
though we both gave each other low blows
There is someone out there who has both our
hearts is it us that's the part
Toxic Tear Drops ....
I know this all may sound absurd,
but these are words that needed to be heard......

~ Journal Thoughts ~

"Toxic Tear Drops"

_____
_____
_____
_____
_____
_____
_____
_____
_____
_____
_____
_____
_____
_____
_____
_____
_____
_____
_____

Where there is no vision, the people perish: but he that keepeth the law, happy is he.

Proverbs 29:18

Life through My Eyes

What I see or is it what I can't see?
Life takes us through unexpected changes, most we can't
prevent
What I see I am not sure if it's meant to be
It's like looking through broken glass wondering how long
is the sight going to last
Watching TV, writing poems, and driving they are all
simple to most but not for me
It's my diagnosis I see
SMH... its gross
What I see through my eyes...
Can't stand nothing bright but the LORD said to me
Sharondla you'll be alright I'm your BACKLIGHT...
You don't see what I see
I see blurred visions
Not a part of my decision to be imprisoned by my own
visions
Viewing the world with one eye
Hmmm. I wonder could I be a spy
A spy that turns back the hands of time to do better with
this health of mine
Diabetes you want all the sweeties and not the Wheaties
well now I eat zucchini...Lol
Frustration when you can't see so well...

Thinking is this my hell
No it can't be, I have much life ahead of me to see
Strong for my daughter I'm trying to be
Already playing the role of mother and father so at times I
pretend it doesn't bother
To think one day I may not see the beautiful woman she's
growing up to be... One eye or two, color has never meant
nothing for me to pursue
My only hope is those with sight will continue to fight for
what is right. Kneeling on someone's throat or being shot
with my hands up
Only provokes the racism in some folks
LORD with the sight that is left to me I hope that the
injustice will soon flee so America can truly be the land of
the FREE...

~ Journal Thoughts ~
"Life Through My Eyes"

_____

_____

_____

_____

_____

_____

_____

_____

_____

_____

_____

_____

_____

_____

_____

_____

_____

_____

Forget the former things; do not dwell on the past. See, I am doing a new thing! Now it springs up; do you not perceive it? I am making a way in the wilderness and streams in the wasteland.

Isaiah 43:18-19

I Got To Let You Go

I got to let you go love

No more wondering if you still care or going to be there

I got to let this burden go so my life can continue to flow

I got to let you go so I see what life is truly about

Mistakes, faults, blame it remains the same but I got to let you go

I've held myself down far too long while you're out carrying on

No more talks of you until I become blue

No more sleepless nights thinking of what I could have done right

But wait it wasn't all me who played the blame game

I got to let you go so my Angel can walk through my door

An Angel who doesn't linger in my past instead grips my hands and becomes my biggest fan

Who will stand with me as we walk through the uncertainty?

I got to let you

I got to heal, In order to kneel

I got to let you go doubt, blame, pain, regret, distrust, you are no longer meant for us

I got to let you so I can be free from the imprisonment I placed upon me

Life goes on, the sun still rises, the wind still blows and God's will for me will be bestowed

I got to let you so Sharondla Patrice Harvey Copes can grow................

~ Journal Thoughts ~

"I Got to Let You Go"

_____

_____

_____

_____

_____

_____

_____

_____

_____

_____

_____

_____

_____

_____

_____

_____

The heart is deceitful above all things, and desperately sick; who can understand it?

Jeremiah 17:9

Feelings Unknown

Why does this always happen to me?
Wanting for someone or something that can't be
I knew what it was from the start I still marched
Open my mind I didn't doubt it at any time
Telling myself I will not fold but your touch I couldn't
control
The heart holds so much and it hurts so much
knowing that you will never be mine
at least not in this lifetime
We both knew what it was from the start but we fit
together like a work of art
You have a life and I knew that from the start
Shit that doesn't mean I want us to be apart
Holding my feelings in when it hurts so much within
Jealousy that can't begin
In the end all I want us to do is win
As I write my heart hurts in the end is it worth ,
worth what I want so bad so I end up sad
Can't talk to you when I want, so I put on a front, like
okay if that's what you want
Knowing all along inside it's like a fire burning my
mind
Something for my soulmate dear god what will it

take
All I want is someone to love I guess I should wait for
you to send it from up above
How will I know when she'll cross my path after all
this aftermath
Pretending that I'm fine but I will come to you at the

drop of a dime
Wondering will my time with you be revoked
because I feel like I'm about to choke?
No one wants to be alone when their grown
We all want to grow old with that one that shapes our
mold
I can express to you how I feel but will you ever know
for real
To be able to speak without being a judge and won't
hold a grudge
These are all pieces of my heart that I and others have
broken apart
Can it ever mend that I don't know where to begin
I try hard to stay out of my head mainly when I lie in
bed
Wondering if I will ever be forgiven for all the pain I
have risen
My emotions are crazy, without a doubt, but it seems
like they are in a bout
Staring off into space wishing we were in a different
place
In a room full of people with my blood flowing
through my veins like others
You tell me you can't be that person, are you for
certain
Loving two people at one time I can say that's fine but
I know I'm lying
I don't want you to make a choice because I know it
was my choice
My choice to love you instead of waiting for someone
new

We both want to let go 'cause we can't choose friend
or foe
No matter how much it hurts I will never treat you
like dirt
You tell me you know what's on my mind or are you
just being kind
Yes I've been hurt before but I only want you more
I feel so free when I'm with you and that's it
I can't be with you...............
Just know I don't want to be apart......

~ Journal Thoughts ~
"Feelings Unknown"

_____

_____

_____

_____

_____

_____

_____

_____

_____

_____

_____

_____

_____

_____

_____

_____

_____

_____

Whoever speaks the truth gives honest evidence, but a false witness utters deceit.

Proverbs 12:17

Greener on the Other Side

In life, we think grass is greener on the other side

until you get there and find it was a bribe

Can't go back on your pride

Hide too many lies from my bride that unlied and

denied the love that was disguised inside …

Let myself get caught up with conversation

I knew it was persuasion

A reaction to the frustrations

Thinking the grass is so much greener should of

stayed in my past and made it last

Now the grass has died

that wasn't advertised but that's what you get

when you subscribe to someone that's not your

design …..

Trying to keep yourself busy with distractions but not

receiving the wanted reactions

Be careful of that green grass it'll have you feeling like

an ass peeping through a looking glass waiting for a

better forecast ……

That grass can't always be greener on the other side …

~ *Journal Thoughts* ~

"Greener on the other Side"

_____

_____

_____

_____

_____

_____

_____

_____

_____

_____

_____

_____

_____

_____

_____

_____

_____

So now faith, hope, and love abide, these three; but the greatest of these is love.

1 Corinthians 13:13

Where Are You Love?

Where are you love?

I turned my back on you too soon

I didn't give you room to breathe or see things through

Where are you love?

Love is the only burden that remains to be seen

Never did I mean to walk out those doors into the unseen

Living life without your love is more difficult than I thought

Life without the one you love

What a halt

Where are you love?

I search for you in darkness and light

Once I find you again love I will never turn or lose you again

Didn't know where I wanted to be but all along it was your love always embracing me

Love where is your beautiful face?

I miss the presence of your Grace

Love, I yearn and scream your name, will you come and release these chains?

Love will you return to me?

Rescue me from this agony

I want our hearts to beat in harmony

Love, will you be so bold, come back and take control

Love, once you arrive again I will never fold, break,
nor bend the vows within

Life without Love, Love without life is living an
impartial life

Love is invisible to me

Love, I remember when we first met, visualizing you
walking up the wooden steps

Dressed in orange and white, Lord what a beautiful
sight

A smile as white as the clouds in the sky

Wondering to myself how could I ever speak the
words goodbye

Who can find a virtuous woman?
For her price is far above rubies.

Proverbs 31:10

Her, Eternal, Respect

HER, where are you: are you close to my heart?

I know you're out there somewhere

Yes someone for me

HER, the woman who knows all my colors

the reds, purples, and blues and every last tattoo

HER, the woman of my equal

that loves me regardless of people

HER, the one I can hand my soul to

HER, the one I need who is not filled with greed

HER, she won't change with time, she seeks the heart

and mind

HER, she deserves all respect

Not any neglect

HER, I have her today Hmmmm will you stay

HER, when you see me

will you come up to greet thee?

HER, in all confidence

You were heaven sent

HER, that all I see that woman brings out courage in

me

who wouldn't desire HER

HER, who craves to be in my presence

then she drains my essences

HER, the one who gives me what I want
the person that genuinely cares about my feelings
that's part of my healing
like she sets her feelings aside to build up my pride
HER, I can call her my own
I never have to wonder when she left alone
physically, mentally, spiritually she will be mine in
due time
Where is she?
In the days to come I hope I won't be numb

~ *Journal Thoughts* ~

"Her, Eternal, Respect"

*And he said, Let me **go**, for the day breaketh. And he said, I will not let thee **go**, except thou bless me.*

Genesis 32:26

I Refuse

No matter what you say I refuse to let you walk away

I just refuse to hear you say we can't play

Girl I refuse to believe that you're not supposed to be

in my life

It just feels so right

I refuse

One day you're going to see that we were truly

meant to be

I refuse to believe she is what you need

When I'm seeing your heart bleed

Yeah maybe its greed but

I refuse to believe that I'm not what you need

The way you stare in my face tells me you want me

all over the place

I Refuse

I Refuse to let this feeling go when I know we can

grow

I never want to be apart but someone else has your

heart

You came into my life but at what price?

Even when we sit in silence my heart beats in vibrant

So should I let you go? It's so much I don't know

I Refuse I Refuse I Refuse

How you walk away then turn around and say are

you okay?

I smile and say

You'll marry me one day

maybe on the beach in May

your favorite spot I remember we used to talk a lot

talk about anything, questions is the fling

but I'm thinking more of engagement rings

I refuse to let go

Just something I needed you to know

~ Journal Thoughts ~

"I Refuse"

_____

_____

_____

_____

_____

_____

_____

_____

_____

_____

_____

_____

_____

_____

_____

_____

_____

_____

_____

*Where there is no **vision**, the people perish: but he that keepeth the law, happy is he.*

Proverbs 29:18

Imagine Me

Imagine me being more than I can be in the eyes of him

Imagine me for once being the child that my parents wanted me to be, Imagine me not being so outspoken when the people you cherish the most secretly wish you the worst

Imagine me having true friends instead of the individuals who pretend

Imagine me loving you honestly instead of engaging in polygamy

Imagine praising the Lord graciously for giving the daughter promised to me

Imagine me expressing these words: worry less

Imagine me rewinding my life just so I can hear my grandmother's voice praying for me at night

Imagine me letting go of every bad experience or feeling of pain go, to allow the love to flow

Imagine me being able to interact with the people like the way I write on paper

Imagine me being judge without grudges

Imagine me having a relationship with all my siblings so fulfilling

Imagine me being free of misery, religious beliefs or political beliefs without giving up the birth rights promised to me

Imagine me being treated the same as others

Imagine giving folks your last and in return their @$$

Imagine me not being so temper matic or dramatic in a society that's systematic

Imagine Me...

~ Journal Thoughts ~
"Imagine Me"

_____
_____
_____
_____
_____
_____
_____
_____
_____
_____
_____
_____
_____
_____
_____
_____
_____
_____
_____
_____
_____

*But I have understanding as well as you; I am not **inferior** to you: yea, who knoweth not such things as these?*

Job 12:3

Inferior to Intimacy

Am I inferior to commitment?

Or maybe I am simply open minded

Love will arise, in the form of it comes

Devotion, won't be the same

Impossibilities of achieving intimacy this is not fiction
the intimacy I am missing

The desires of a family to display humanity

Attracted to your body's physical physique makes me
weak

Visualizing warm kisses placed upon my forehead
anticipating the intimacy which lies ahead

In my thoughts I am not attractive enough for you,
the jealousy sets in........ Inferior to you (Intimacy)

~ Journal Thoughts ~
"Inferior to Intimacy"

_____

_____

_____

_____

_____

_____

_____

_____

_____

_____

_____

_____

_____

_____

_____

_____

_____

_____

_____

_____

*Be **strong** and of a good courage, fear not, nor be afraid of them: for the L*ORD *thy God, he it is that doth go with thee; he will not fail thee, nor forsake thee.*

Deuteronomy 31:6

Pieces of Me

I break, I bend, I've been put back together again

You would think after so many times my mind would
or should be wise
Pieces of me that are piece (peace) in me
Lying in my bed with so many thoughts swarming in
my
head thinking of what lies ahead
Pieces of me.....
Holding on to the past lord, how long until the last?
Its time to move on shit you know how many times

I've sang that song Shrugs .....

Pieces of me.......
Its time I get back my self-control so I can
setup my stepping stone
Time to show my seat that in life we will grieve
but it's not the last leaf you will succeed
Pieces of me that should of never been shown has
made me grown
Learn experiences that will remain remembrances
lingers in my brain like a freight train but then

I think to myself you got to think about your health
Pieces of me.....
It's not about your looks or what you buy it's those

feelings when we look into each other eyes

Days seem different, nights are long, but still
I have to remain strong
Strong beautiful black queen that's strong
to gain her wings and will survive by any means
Pieces of me........
I will RISE UP even if I have to do it
a thousand times by speaking life and encouraging
myself through these rhymes of mine......
Pieces of me....

~ Journal Thoughts ~
"Pieces of Me"

_____

_____

_____

_____

_____

_____

_____

_____

_____

_____

_____

_____

_____

_____

_____

_____

_____

_____

_____

_____

*To everything there is a season, and a **time** to every purpose under the heaven: A **time** to be born, and a **time** to die; a **time** to plant, and a **time** to pluck up that which is planted; A **time** to kill, and a **time** to heal; a **time** to break down, and a **time** to build up;*

Ecclesiastes 3:1-3

Moments

Moments we have so many of them
Moments of where I want to feel my fingers in your
hair when we are both bare
Moments that are so perfect that a picture can't make
it perfect

Moments where I can feel your hands running up my
thigh as my body fights and says "oh my"
Moments when I feel I can't live without you
Moments when I can't stand being around you
Moments when my body burns and yearns only
makes my mind be more concerned

Moments when I want you the most and I turn and
you're a ghost
Moments when I pretend that I'm in control but it's
just a front to show you I'm bold
Moments when I feel like I can't breathe when you
leave but I know you will give me something much
more to achieve
You give me a much brighter feeling in my daily
living

Moments Moments Moments
I wish I could have all your moments but I know
there are other components

Moments when I don't have to pretend to be the
person within

Moments when I'm not a judge even if I wanted to be
stud
Lol Lol

Yeah those moments that make me laugh before you
feel my rapt smiles

Moments when I can be completely free that's when
you bring the best of me

Moments when I don't feel so good within, then
you look at me and say let's begin

Let's begin this journey that's sent from above
Hmmm it has so much love
Moments that none of us can live without because
there is no other route

Moments where I get tired then I look at you and get
inspired

Moments like these are really all I need

~ Journal Thoughts ~
"Moments"

_____
_____
_____
_____
_____
_____
_____
_____
_____
_____
_____
_____
_____
_____
_____
_____
_____
_____
_____
_____

*And you will know the truth, and
the truth will set you free.*

John 8:32

My

My first, My last, My gain, placing these words on paper
of My hurt, My flirt, My love, my hate, My shame , My
game, My failure , My success, My age, My gender, My
color

My beginning, My end, My friend , My enemy, My lane,
My depression, My joy, My happiness, My heart, My tears,
My light, My darkness, My regret, My feelings of not
feeling humane……

My feelings of going insane , My woman , My wife, My
presence, My past, my hopes, my dreams of fame, my
daughter , my world, my girl, my addiction, my abuse, my
sadness, my lifestyle, my lies emotions deeply engraved.

My confessions, inspirations, truths. My anger, more pain,
my health , my God, my emotions, my mind frame, my
wisdom, my poems, my moment , my appearance, my
anointing, my blame, my sweat, my blood, my praise, my
burdens, my song, my preacher, my gain, my change, my
voice, my vision, my life, my Bible translates to say that
my gift will make room for me…..

Proverbs 18:16

~ Journal Thoughts ~
"My"

$ Money $

Do you see what's truly hidden within me or do you see the green scenery surrounding me?

Trying too desperately for people to see the good in me

Something I decline to see

So, I provide the only element they seek "mean green" which created curiosity, envy, and jealousy

Wondering if I didn't have the money these darks clouds would be sunny

So I am on my knees on Sundays praying for more money……..Dummy

Would people still cling to me like a leech or drop like flies when the money is no longer in reach?

Money when I have it humans are like honey

Family versus Friends…… Scummy

Hamm... Too funny but instead it feels crummy

When am I only seen when I have money

Money, can I speak my mind or should I just give in then go and hide, hide my feelings of abuse and pain so others can rain on my reign…

Questioning myself whether people love me because of the
potential wealth

If they only knew that the green means absolutely nothing
to thee

But it seems the green is the reason, I am seen.....

(Greed)

Proverbs 13:11

~ Journal Thoughts ~
"Money"

Author's Favorite Quotes

"I'm selfish, impatient, and a little insecure. I make mistakes, I am out of control and, at times, hard to handle.

But if you can't handle me at my worst, then you sure as hell don't deserve me at my best."

Marilyn Monroe

"If you can't figure out your purpose, figure out your passion."

Bishop T.D. Jakes

"I've learned that people will forget what you said, people will forget what you did, but people will never forget how you made them feel."

Maya Angelou

"Sometimes it is not the conflict that triggers emotional pain, but the SILENCE. Blocking, avoiding, ignoring, neglecting loved ones can be just as abusive as verbal attacks. Control can be through non-action too."

Kelly Martin

Parent Tribute

I would like to pay tribute to my mother and father. I dedicate this book to the both of you. I realize in life that parents are the foundation for a child's life journey. Although we may have not always seen eye to eye in everything in my life I take today to honor you for being my parents and instilling in me some of the qualities I possess today. Each one of you have contributed some seeds into my garden of life and from them I have watched myself grow in areas I thought would never manifest. This book I birth is a collection of my thoughts, feelings, and spiritual energy that rest on the inside of me.

I pray you are as proud of me for this accomplishment as I am of myself.

Conclusion

Confessions, Inspirations, and Truth is a collection of my poetry that was manufactured from my soul. It is a raw representation of the things my mind, body, and soul have accumulated over the years. It is the raw portion of my hurt and pain as well as a clear picture of my struggles and sacrifices. I confess through my writings my own personal truths. I write from my own sense of self. I write from the perspective that lingers deep within my soul.

My goal is that someone would be inspired to face the hurdles of life that they too face and be able to look themselves square in the eyes and declare the truth as they know it.

I write to bring awareness to others who may have had to deny themselves for the sake of others, I write to free myself from the stereotypes hinged upon me. I write to declare freedom from the bondage of not being good enough.

I wanted to tell my story through my poetry. I pray that this poetic journey has touched your life in some sort of way and you will begin to reflect on the challenges you face and decide to free yourself from the bondages of life. Make a conscious effort today to confess your personal truths and be okay with how the world views it. Use what you have experienced and learned in life to inspire others.

About the Author

Sharondla Harvey was born on August 22, 1980 in Gainesville, Florida to the parents of Sandra Moore and Freddie Harvey. Sharondla was raised in the small town of Williston, Florida with her mother and grandmother Doeretha Robinson who instilled the power of God in her which led to her own personal relationship with God today. Sharondla has a daughter name Mckenzie Jackson who she is dedicating this book of poetry to. Sharondla has been creating poetry since her adolescent years. Shalonda's writings are inspired by her life experiences of pain, shame, regret, and struggles with identity of herself. Sharondla currently resides in Jacksonville, Florida where she continues to create poetry because in life we as human beings all have a story or stories to share which she calls Confessions, Truths, and Inspiration.

Author's Contact Page

Facebook : Sharondla Harvey

IG: Sharondla Harvey

Made in the USA
Columbia, SC
03 October 2023

23341489R00050